Richness in Christ

Chuck Tooman

248.4 T618r
Tooman, Chuck.
Richness in Christ

*"Making ready a
people for the Lord."*
Luke 1:17

**2121 Barnes Avenue SE
Salem, OR 97306 USA**

Copyright ©2006
by Chuck Tooman

First Printing, May 2006

Published by

PREPARING THE WAY
Publishers

**2121 Barnes Avenue SE
Salem, OR 97306 USA**

All rights reserved. No part of this book may be reproduced, translated, stored in a retrieval system or transmitted in any form by any means, whether electronic, mechanical, photocopying, recording or otherwise, without prior written permission from the copyright holder.

All Scripture quotations taken from the *Holy Bible*, New Living Translation, copyright 1996. Used by permission of Tyndale House Publishers, Inc., Wheaton, Illinois 60189. All rights reserved.

ISBN 1-929451-20-2
Library of Congress Catalog Card Number 2006901934

Printed in the United States of America

Dedication

This book is most gratefully dedicated to those followers of Jesus Christ who have so greatly influenced my life.

About the Author

I was born in the late 30's, and my sister Judy and I spent our growing up years on a small farm in northern Indiana. There was no electricity or running water. The roof leaked and the cold came in, but the one thing that was never missing was love.

Our father Earl worked the second shift in a munitions factory. So every night at bedtime our mother Belva read us a Bible story, helped us with prayers, and tucked us safely into bed. The house was small and the flickering of the flame from the lone kerosene lamp on the kitchen table, casting its golden glow into the bedroom where we slept, is among my warmest memories. Dad and Mom are both now safely home in heaven

We went to town three times a week—Saturday nights for groceries and shopping, Sundays for church and Sunday school, and Wednesday Evening Prayer. That was a given because someone always came from town to give us a ride.

At age 12 I walked down the aisle to give my heart to Jesus, and was baptized that same evening. At age 15, while at church camp, I felt God put a call on my life to become a missionary/pastor. Throughout high school and the army I was committed to that calling. My strong and confident faith brought me through lots of challenges—school, athletics, the army, several leadership positions, and well into college.

During my senior year of college, however, life began to unravel, even though I was not aware of it at the time. Rather than pursuing the mission field, or ministry, I told myself, "I can minister in many ways," and changed my major to education. Not long after I began to get a haunting feeling that one day there would be a time of reckoning.

The years from 22 to 40 were years of moves, jobs, and searching. Teaching, counseling, publishing, community service and ulcers were among my common activities. Even though things usually seemed right on the outside, inside was a different story. Life would work out, almost. There would be peace, but not quite. Always a restless searching. I drifted away from church at times but was always aware of a tugging that would not let go.

One night at age 39, in the midst of a crisis, I surrendered. "Okay, Lord. You know where I am, you know what I can do, I am listening." I knew in that moment that I was headed for the ministry. I did not know how, when, or where. That was God's business, and I trusted Him to provide. I do know that I slept that night in a way that I had not slept in a long time. The year was 1977. Within a year I was in the ministry full time.

For the next 26 years God taught me about prayer, healing, fasting, praise, worship, a pioneering spirit, planting churches, the Holy Spirit, and the power of His Word.

At age 54 I began to develop two diseases that at age 60 would cause me to become almost dysfunctional. One night, at a worship celebration in Connecticut, a Nigerian evangelist prayed over me, and through the ministry of the Holy Spirit I was instantly healed.

Since that time I have prayed over others and seen the Holy Spirit heal many of them instantly, or a healing experience begun. Twice within the recent past, within a ninety-day period, I was told, "You have cancer." Today, two surgeries and many powerful prayers later, doctors tell me I am cancer-free.

When Jesus healed people they immediately rejoiced and began to tell others what Jesus had done in their lives. The Spirit has laid it upon my heart to do the same.

What difference does Jesus make in my life? Jesus has made all the difference in my life. He provides all my needs. He comforts me in times of sorrow. He awakens in me a desire to live a pure and holy life. He helps me resolve my problems. He heals me when I get sick. He keeps me from the snares of the devil. He helps me forgive those who hurt me. He gives me wisdom and direction in the decisions of life. He reveals truth to me when I read the Bible. He enables me to teach, to share the Good News of God's love with others. He gives me strength to reach out and help those in need. I am thankful that I heard the simple message of God's love and forgiveness at an early age and gave my heart to Jesus.

In January of 2002, my wife Barb and I made this covenant with God: "Lord Jesus, our lives are totally and completely yours for the fulfilling of the Great Commission in our time. Whenever, wherever, however, regardless of the cost. We are yours. Chuck and Barb Tooman." We wrote it, we each signed it, and then lifted it up to Him in prayer. Again, I say there is no life like the surrendered life, and once you have tasted it you cannot live any other way.

Foreword

I meet a lot of godly people in the ministry of missionary evangelism and church planting, but I have never met anyone with a deeper devotion to Jesus Christ than Chuck Tooman! He is a man of unquestioned integrity and solid commitment to the Lord and to the work of the Lord. He and his wife Barb are models of Christian commitment both as individuals and as a married couple.

I first met Chuck and Barb when they invited me to minister in their church in Marquette, Michigan, on the subject of church planting . . . house church planting. They were pastors of a traditional church at the time, which they had founded several years before and were in the process of resigning that position to fulfill a vision from the Lord to plant one thousand house churches.

I have been amazed at how beautifully they were able to make that transition without causing a major explosion with a lot of messy fallout! How successful they were in this venture was apparent to me when, a few years later, after Chuck had resigned as pastor and had begun planting house churches, he invited me to conduct another house church seminar in Marquette and we were invited to use the facilities of the church where Chuck was formerly pastor! That is something of a miracle in itself, but it also shows a God-given anointing resting on Chuck's life and ministry!

Chuck and I got a lot better acquainted when the Lord led us to do a multi-state missionary journey about a year ago doing house church conferences and seminars. I was even more impressed with this man of God by the time we had completed that outreach!

If anyone in the Body of Christ is qualified to write on the riches we have inherited in Christ, it is Chuck Tooman! I have enjoyed many days of hospitality in the Tooman home on various occasions and I can say that Chuck and Barb daily live out the gospel they preach and teach.

I am sure that by reading this book, you will glean some of the riches that God has poured into their lives over the many years they have been walking with Jesus in their home, their workplace, and their outreach into all the world through a ministry they have founded called Christ's Servants to the Nations.

The scripture that comes to my mind when I think of the life and ministry of Chuck Tooman is 2 Corinthians 4:5, "For we preach not ourselves, but Christ Jesus the Lord; and ourselves your servants for Jesus' sake" (KJV).

~ Robert Fitts
Kailua-Kona, Hawaii

Preface

Every day, in my role as a hospice chaplain, I spend time with people who are at one of the most precious points of their lives—they are within six months, more or less, of dying. People who know they are dying go through something called EOL—end of life review. EOL often involves lots of pain—spiritual pain—and spiritual pain can be just as painful as physical pain. Sometimes spiritual pain even exacerbates physical pain. The difference is that there is no pill for spiritual pain.

Spiritual pain comes from such things as hopelessness, fear, loss, failure, finally accepting that some dreams won't be completed, some relationships will not be reconciled. All are symptoms of separation from God and a lack of intimacy with His Son Jesus Christ.

The sad thing about most spiritual pain is that it did not have to happen. This book is written in part for those not yet facing EOL, those who have time yet to make choices and adjustments that will allow their EOL to be a celebration of life rather than feeling they have failed at life.

One thing we often fail to understand is that we are created to live forever. We were conceived in the Father's heart in eternity past, on His timing we arrived in eternity present, and in His timing we will transition into eternity future. Dying is the way we transition from this life into the next life. We take nothing from this life into the next—everything is worked out and taken care of before we leave here. Our Richness in Christ is about living all of life for all of life—about preparing for that transition to be a time of joy and celebration rather than regret and despair.

Through richness in Christ we can truly live all of life for all of life.

Contents

	Introduction	15
1.	Where and How Does Richness in Christ Begin?	21
2.	Richness in Christ and the Journey into Community	25
3.	Richness in Christ and Cornerstone Communities	29
4.	Richness in Christ and Decision Time	33
5.	Richness in Christ and the Journey into Grace	35
6.	Intimacy and Richness	39
7.	My Response to Jesus' Call to Richness and Intimacy	43
8.	Three Essentials to Richness in Christ and Cornerstone Communities	47
9.	Richness in Christ and Finishing Well	49
10.	Richness and My Core Purpose	55
11.	Cornerstone Communities and the Shield of Faith	57
12.	Richness in Christ and Church Pure and Holy	59
13.	A Simple Plan for Experiencing Richness in Christ with Others	63
14.	Sustaining Richness in Christ	65
15.	Richness in Christ and the Power of the Blood of Jesus	69
	A Terrible Urgency	73
	Bibliography	75
	Additional Books from PTWP	77

Introduction

Come to Christ, who is the living cornerstone of God's temple. He was rejected by the people, but he is precious to God who chose him. And now God is building you, as living stones, into His spiritual temple . . . for you are a chosen people. You are a kingdom of priests, God's holy nation, his very own possession. This is so you can show others the goodness of God, for he called you out of the darkness into his wonderful light (1 Peter 2:4, 5a, 9).

In 68 years of living I have learned that when Jesus is the cornerstone of one's life the Jesus Journey is...

- A life worth living.

   Other journeys result in empty, meaningless lives.

- A love worth finding.

   Only Jesus' love does not leave us hungering and thirsting for more.

- A peace worth having.

   It is the complete answer to restless hearts.

- A faith worth walking.

   If we do not stand strong for faith, we will not stand for anything at all.

- A risk worth taking.

   It is an investment only in things eternal.

- A price worth paying.

  Jesus' love is the only love that totally surrounds us with God's wisdom, grace, peace, mercy, and all other attributes of God's character every moment of every day no matter what our circumstance

I've also learned that Cornerstone lives produce Cornerstone homes and communities and that Cornerstone homes and communities are the safest places on earth.

In Cornerstone homes and communities...

- People feel warmly loved, highly valued, deeply respected, greatly encouraged, and genuinely supported—even in tough times.
- Relationships make a difference and set an example.
- People and relationships withstand life's storms.
- Dreams, visions, and goals are allowed and encouraged.
- People bring out the best in each other.
- Joy is present, even in the midst of heartaches.
- People and relationships are forgiven and restored.
- People think and value in terms of eternity, not just the present.
- Life is not perfect, but it is very good.
- Jesus Christ is the center.

My passion is for every home everywhere to be a cornerstone home, and for every person everywhere to be a part of a Cornerstone Community.

On July 23, 2005, I received this commission:

> Chuck, I have set you on the Jesus Journey and given you the concept of Cornerstone Homes and Cornerstone Communities. Now, bring it all together through *Richness in Christ*, the richness that comes only through Christ Jesus—My Son. For in Him alone lie hidden all the treasures of wisdom and knowledge. You are complete when you are in union with Christ. He is Lord over every ruler and authority in the universe.
>
> Chuck, take the message of the richness of Christ to the world. All the rest will fall into place. Focus on the richness of Christ and the power of the cross. The homes and the communities will then come together.

Note to the reader: Cornerstone Homes is not a movement or an attempt to start a denomination. It is a concept. Oswald Chambers has written, "The Church ceases to be a spiritual society when it is on the lookout for the development of its own organization." Enough said.

The commissioning then created a yearning

There was a yearning in the Spirit's word and voice as he spoke the following to me:

> Chuck, be the richness of Christ to others. Let them experience through you how long, how wide, how high, how deep my love really is. Let the fruit of my Spirit always be present in you: love, joy, peace, patience, kindness, gentleness, goodness, faithfulness, and self-control.
>
> Clothe yourself in tenderhearted mercy, kindness, humility, gentleness and patience. Make allowances for others' faults and forgive those who

offend you. I forgave you so you must forgive them. Make love the most important piece of clothing you have to wear, for love is what binds the church together in perfect harmony. Let the peace of Christ rule in your heart and make you wise. And always be thankful. Use my words to teach and counsel others. And whatever you do or say, let it be as a representative of the Lord Jesus, all the while giving thanks through him to God the Father.

Live wisely among those who are not Christians, and make the most of every opportunity. Let your conversation be gracious and effective so that you will have the right answer for everyone.

This should be your ambition: to live a quiet life, minding your own business. As a result, people who are not Christians will respect the way you live, and you will not need to depend on others for your financial needs.

Always be full of joy in the Lord. Let everyone see that you are considerate in all that you do. Don't worry about anything; instead, pray about everything. Tell God what you need and don't forget to thank Him for His answers. If you do this, you will experience God's peace, which is far more wonderful than the human mind can understand. His peace will guard your heart and your mind as you live in Christ Jesus.

Worship Christ as the Lord of your life. And if you are asked about your Christian hope, always be ready to explain it. But do it in a gentle and respectful way, keeping your conscience clear. Then if people speak evil against you, they will be ashamed when they see what a good life you live because you belong to Christ.

Again Chuck, be the richness of Christ to others.

Words That Burn in My Heart

As I listened to the Spirit's yearning and urging and pleading there were words that burned in my heart, words from deep in the soil of God's marvelous love...

> Oh, what a wonderful God we have! How great are his riches and wisdom and knowledge! How impossible it is for us to understand his decisions and his methods! For who can know what the Lord is thinking? Who knows enough to be his counselor? And who could ever give him so much that he would have to pay it back? For everything comes from him; everything exists by his power and is intended for his glory. To him be glory evermore. Amen (Romans 11:33-36).

> When I think of the wisdom and scope of God's plan, I fall to my knees and pray to the Father, the Creator of everything in heaven and on earth. I pray that from his glorious, unlimited resources he will give you mighty inner strength through his Holy Spirit. And I pray that Christ will be more and more at home in your hearts as you trust in him. May your roots go down deep into the soil of God's marvelous love. And may you have the power to understand, as all God's people should, how wide, how long, how high, and how deep his love really is. May you experience the love of Christ, though it is so great you will never fully understand it. Then you will be filled with the fullness of life and power that comes from God (Ephesians 3:14-19).

> Since God chose you to be the holy people whom he loves, you must clothe yourselves with tenderhearted mercy, kindness, humility, gentleness, and patience. You must make allowance for each other's faults and forgive the person who offends you. Remember, the Lord forgave you, so you must forgive others. And the most important piece of clothing you must wear is

love. Love is what binds us all together in perfect harmony. And let the peace that comes from Christ rule in your hearts. For as members of one body you are all called to live in peace. And always be thankful. Let the words of Christ, in all their richness, live in your hearts and make you wise. Use his words to teach and counsel each other. Sing psalms and hymns and spiritual songs to God with thankful hearts. 17And whatever you do or say, let it be as a representative of the Lord Jesus, all the while giving thanks through him to God the Father (Colossians 3:12-17).

But the wisdom that comes from heaven is first of all pure. It is also peace loving, gentle at all times, and willing to yield to others. It is full of mercy and good deeds. It shows no partiality and is always sincere (James 3:17).

one

Where and How Does Richness in Christ Begin?

Where does richness in Christ begin? It began long ago—in the heart of the Father. Even before the creation of the world.

Not only did I exist in the Father's heart, He also had a purpose for me. In fact, He knew the very moment He would birth me out of His heart and into the world so that I might fulfill the purpose for which He created and conceived me. My life and my purpose were conceived in the Father's heart long before I was conceived in the world, to begin my walk with Jesus and to live in richness with him.

But there's more. When I was conceived in the Father's heart He cared about me so much that He placed within my heart all the richness of His heart, so that when I became all He created and conceived me to be, would be fully expressed in the world around me. The richness of His heart would be expressed through my heart. Such things as love, joy, peace, patience, kindness, gentleness, faithfulness, goodness and self-control. And not just love, but the fullness of His love.

How humble, unworthy yet honored I feel.

Yet, there's more. In the Bible the Father tells me that throughout my earthly journey the Spirit of the Sovereign Lord will be upon me, and that He trusts me so much that He has appointed me to bring good news to the poor. He has sent me to comfort the broken-hearted and to announce freedom to the spiritual captives that they will be released and the prisoners in bondage will be freed. He says that His will for me is a crown of beauty instead of ashes, the oil of gladness instead of mourning, and a garment of praise instead of a spirit of despair. He says I'll be an oak of righteousness, a planting of His own for the display of his splendor.

He created me in His heart with a never-ending love, a wonderful purpose, and a faithfulness that endures forever. Oh, the depth of the riches and the wisdom of his knowledge. How unsearchable his judgments, and his paths are beyond tracing out!

How can I ever respond! I can only respond as others responded before me: When I think of the wisdom and scope of the Father's plan, I fall to my knees and pray to the Father, the Creator of everything in heaven and on earth! I pray that from His glorious, unlimited resources He will give me mighty inner strength through his Holy Spirit. I pray that Jesus Christ will be more and more at home in my heart as I trust in him. I pray that my roots will go down deep into the soil of God's marvelous love. I pray that I may have the power to understand, as all God's people should, how wide, how long, how high, and how deep his love really is. I pray to experience the love of Christ, though it is so great I will never fully understand it. I pray to be filled with the fullness of life and power that comes from the Father, for I know that by His mighty power at work within us, He is able to accomplish infinitely more than we would ever dare to ask or hope. I pray that He be given glory in the church and in Christ Jesus forever and ever through endless ages.

That's my response.

And since the Father chose me to be a holy person whom He loves, I clothe myself with tenderhearted mercy, kindness, humility, gentleness, and patience. I seek to make allowance for others' faults and forgive the person who offends me. The Lord forgave me, so I must forgive others. And the most important piece of clothing I can wear is love for love is what binds us all together in perfect harmony. And I pray for the peace that comes from Christ to rule in my heart...for we are all called to live in peace. And to always be thankful.

And as I walk the Jesus journey may the words of Christ, in all their richness, live in my heart and make me wise. May I use His words to teach and counsel others. May I sing psalms and hymns and spiritual songs to God with a thankful heart. And whatever I do or say, may it be as a representative of the Lord Jesus, all the while giving thanks through him to God the Father.

That's where the journey with Jesus and richness in Christ begin. In me...my heart...my home, my walk. My moment-by-moment walk with Jesus. Not that I may live simply as a Christian, but as one created long ago in the heart of the Father that His Son Jesus may live in and through me to the glory of the Father. Amen!

two

Richness in Christ and the Journey into Community

There is a point at which the journey into richness takes us outside ourselves and into community. It just happened again. It's Saturday afternoon. I'm sitting at the computer, alone with my thoughts. Reflecting. Barb came into the room just as I was beginning to sob and cry my heart out over some issues that had been building for some time and were really tearing at my heart. For awhile she just held me while I sobbed. Then as I began to quiet down, she sat down on the floor next to my chair and simply, quietly, compassionately said, "Talk to me." And I did. Without reservation or fear I just poured it all out while she compassionately entered into my pain and listened. It was a time when our hearts were one.

The journey into richness is not to be walked alone; it is to be walked together. It's about bearing one another's burdens. It is about oneness with others, about learning community. And living in community. The Kingdom of God is community-based and is lived out through richness in Christ. Jesus said, *"Where two or three are gathered in my name, I am there with them."* Heaven itself is community-based: *"In my Father's house are many rooms..."*

The Jesus Journey is also community-based: *"Love one*

another. As I have loved you, so you must love one another."

For me, the place where love, community, Kingdom and richness in Christ begin to deepen, and take on substance and meaning, is marriage—the uniting of two hearts into one.

Marriage is the means by which beauty breaks forth into the world. It is where church begins. It is where all those things God placed within us at conception are given expression, are nurtured, finely-tuned and then joyfully burst forth onto the landscape of our lives. The uniting of one man and one woman is the primary earthly relationship. It is where love, joy, peace, patience, gentleness, kindness, faithfulness, goodness, and self-control are given flesh.

Marriage is where we learn that commitment means living with the results. We learn the strength and truth of living in community, and are encouraged for the journey. It is where we learn lessons that apply to all of life for we learn the price and the rewards of "for better or worse, for richer or poorer, in sickness and in health until one shall lay the other into the arms of the Lord." The extent to which we are faithful to that we experience richness in Christ, and the Kingdom of God is present. If we handle marriage well, we'll also handle community and Kingdom well.

Next to Jesus, Barb and I are the center of each other's lives and a precious presence at the core of each other's being. We seek to love each other as Christ loves us and are ready to pay whatever price that commitment exacts. We are at times tempted and buffeted by all kinds of realities and circumstances. Yet at the same time we know that we can do all things through Christ who strengthens us. We know that we can live by the promise that every child of God defeats this evil world by trusting Christ to give the victory, and we know that those who win the victories over this world are those who believe that Jesus is the Son of God, for in Christ lie hidden all the treasures of wisdom and knowledge.

"Where two or three are gathered in my name I am there with them." The integrity of living this out in our marriage is crucial to the integrity of the rest of the journey because integrity begins with me, in my own home, and in my own marriage. If integrity is not fully present here, then neither will community nor the Kingdom of God be present. If integrity is not fully present in my relationship with Barb, it will not be present in my relationship with others. I will never experience richness in Christ, and I will never be a cornerstone in anyone's foundation, an issue we'll pursue in just a few pages.

Marriage is...

>A life worth living
>A love worth finding
>A peace worth having
>A faith worth walking
>A risk worth taking
>A price worth paying

For marriage is community, Kingdom, church and richness in Christ in its purest form...and opens the door to the rest of the journey.

three

Richness in Christ and Cornerstone Communities

The cornerstone is the most important stone, or block, in the foundation of a building. It is the stone on which everything else depends; the stone that makes the difference.

Deep down inside, in the middle of the night, when my heart and mind are quiet and open to receiving, there is a calling and a drawing and an aching to be a living cornerstone—to make a difference. To truly and fully become what I was created to become even before the foundation of the world. I don't have a desire to build an empire or a dynasty; I just want to be sure that my life counts for something. I desire the peace of knowing that in the final analysis I have given everything I am to that which is solid, trustworthy, and eternal. I desire that because Jesus calls us to *bear fruit*, and the fruit He calls us to bear is Christ-likeness. In fact, He says that His true followers will bear much fruit. I desire to be a fruit-bearing cornerstone because it is consistent with what God the Father has created and called me to be. He has planted His character within us and has set eternity in all our hearts.

In order to be a living cornerstone I need to surrender

my life to some thing or some one much greater than I am, and to allow that person or thing to passionately direct everything about me. In the very center of my being I need to feel at peace about to whom and what I am surrendered to. If I am to be a cornerstone, then my life needs to be surrendered to the One who creates cornerstones.

Today, I am able to peacefully and joyfully say that my heart has found that which fulfills my desire and longing to make a difference, count for something, and touch the lives of others in a truly meaningful way. It is not a thing; it is a relationship with a person—Jesus Christ. And I don't have to go looking for it; it just happens.

Let me explain. In the beginning God created the heavens and the earth. God also created people, and His innermost desire was that people would reflect His own image. People, however, rejected what God had created them to be. God then sent His Son Jesus to earth to show people how to live, and to be an example of what God is really like.

People, however, rejected Jesus and put Him to death by nailing Him to a cross. But God loved His people so much that still He would not give up on them. So God determined that the wounds in Jesus' body and the blood running from those wounds would be for the cleansing and the forgiveness of the sins of the whole world, for all people for all time, if only they would receive His Son Jesus as the center of their lives.

Jesus was buried in a tomb but three days later defeated death by arising from that tomb and once again living among God's people. Today, Jesus is in heaven, sitting at the right hand of God the Father Almighty, Maker of Heaven and Earth.

But there is more. In defeating death and living a new life, Jesus also made it possible for us to defeat the things that would crucify and bury us in order that we, too, may live new lives. God said that the way that would happen is for Jesus to be the cornerstone of our lives and for us to be living stones whose lives reflect Jesus, the cornerstone. Jesus is present and living among us today in the person of his Spirit. He desires to live in relationship with us, and offers us everything we need to live cornerstone lives.

Jesus Christ is Lord and Master of my life and is everything I need to live a life that truly counts. He gives meaning, purpose, and direction to my every moment, and I can truly and completely be at peace and rest in Him for now and for eternity regardless of the turmoil that may be going on around me. Jesus is at the core of my being. He is life abundant in the midst of all that would kill and destroy me and render me useless, lifeless, non-existent. He is light in the darkness, peace in the tempest, direction in the midst of uncertainty, strength in weakness, relationship in the midst of loneliness, and ever so much more.

I desire Jesus to be the cornerstone of my life, and I desire my home to be a cornerstone home. I desire my life, my home, my relationships to be a light, message, invitation, and example to the world around me. I desire to live in Christ-likeness, and I know that if I do that, if I surrender everything about me to Jesus Christ, then He will direct my steps and my path toward things that count, make a difference, and are eternal.

What about you? What is your desire? Do you, too, long for significance and to know that your life counts for something? Do you wish to know a peace that passes understanding? Do you seek a quiet restfulness that is just indescribable regardless of all around you that seeks to destroy peace and rest? Do you desire to experience richness in Christ?

I invite you to pray this prayer with me:

> Lord Jesus, I am tired of life as it has been. I'm tired of turmoil, emptiness, uncertainty, and all else that is often part of my embattled life. I desire relationships that are real and a purpose that is eternal and right in Your eyes. In short, I want to surrender my life to You. Totally and completely I give myself to You, trusting You and You alone to lead me in a life that is pleasing to You. Help me to know and be a living stone that reflects You as the cornerstone. And lead me to relationships that will be pleasing and strengthening as I walk my journey with You. Help me to walk a Jesus journey, to live a cornerstone life in cornerstone community. Thank you, Jesus. Thank you, Lord.

Cornerstone lives cannot be lived alone. Cornerstone lives need cornerstone communities—other people who are also committed to Jesus Christ. I am a hospice chaplain. Every day I hear dying people and their loved ones review their lives. The place they all come to, when all is said and done, is that living a life centered on Jesus is really all that matters. Everything else is loss.

That is why God's message to me is,

> Chuck, I have given you the cause—God first in the nations. I have given you the heart and core of cornerstone living—the Jesus Journey—the Way, the Truth, and the Life. America will never be fully restored and will never fully reveal My light and My glory to the nations until it walks with My Son Jesus. Now, I am giving you the process—cornerstone communities of cornerstone people walking the Jesus journey. You have all you need. Take it to the nations.

four

Richness in Christ and Decision Time

Moses said, "Who, me?"

Jonah said, "Not me."

Habakkuk said, "Why me?"

Isaiah said, "Send me."

In the Book of Esther, at a time of great peril and potential annihilation for the entire Jewish race, Mordecai said to Queen Esther, *"Who knows but what you were born for a time such as this?"* Esther responded to a need for unprecedented action in that time of great peril by saying *"If I perish, I perish."* Through Esther's courage the traitor Haman was unmasked and the nation was saved.

Patrick Henry is well-known for his freedom cry during the early days of the American Revolution, *"I know not what course others may choose, but as for me give me liberty or give me death."*

The world is desperate for people who walk in richness with Christ.

Every home and nation on earth, as solid or great as they

may seem, lives in a time of great spiritual and moral crises and desperately needs those who will stand for truth and not sell out to the enemy. Our homes and nations need those who will stand before God on their knees and say, as did Isaiah (6:8), *"Here am I, send me."* The world needs those who will stand before God and say in their hearts, "Maybe I was born for a time such as this." God calls out for people who are willing to pay the price, who are surrendered to Him and willing to lead without reservation. In short, the world needs people who are willing to pay the price of walking in richness with Christ.

We are in a time of great spiritual warfare and we need those who are willing to stand against spiritual chains and spiritual slavery and say, "I know not what course others may choose, but as for me, give me liberty or give me death."

What's your price?!

- What price are you willing to pay? Will you stand for truth?
- Are you willing to defend the flock against false shepherds and self-serving leaders?
- Are you willing to consider that perhaps you were born for a time such as this?
- Are you willing to pay the price for helping homes and nations return to their moral and spiritual roots by walking the Jesus journey yourself? By leading a cornerstone community?

Are you prepared to proclaim in this time of great spiritual darkness, as you lead others into the light of truth, "Here am I. Send me."? If so, you will find all the strength you need in your richness in Christ.

five

Richness in Christ
and
The Journey into Grace

Grace: *The Kindness of God toward man.*

We said earlier that if we handle marriage well, we'll handle community and Kingdom well. One of the truths of life is that the manner in which we live out the marriage relationship can establish a pattern for handling the rest of life. If we bail out on the *tough stuff* of marriage, we'll be prone to bail out of other tough stuff as well. Bailing out keeps community and Kingdom from happening and can greatly diminish our journey into richness in Christ.

Some marriages succeed gloriously. Some try and fail. Others try, fail, try a second time, and finally break through all the bondages that keep *"greater love has no man than to lay down his life for a friend"* from happening.

Barb and I are a second-marriage. All that looked good on the outside in our previous marriages turned out to have some hollowness on the inside—first in the people, then in the couples. Life got *off track*. Things were not handled well; things that denied God's Holy Spirit full expression. As a second-marriage couple we have occasionally experienced disapproval from some, even closed doors to ministry. For a rare few we are the woman caught in adultery and brought before Jesus for judgment, and it seems that in almost every crowd there are those who can hardly wait to throw stones.

But that's where grace steps in. Grace, as in Jesus. Grace, as in the kindness of God toward fallen people. Grace, as in Jesus the only person present who was qualified to throw a stone but didn't. Jesus simply said that He wasn't condemning us, just don't let it happen again. Then He invited us to resume the journey with Him. That's richness.

Now in our twenty-third year of marriage Jesus Christ is the center of our lives. We are people redeemed by the shed blood of Jesus on the cross, and we are committed to community and Kingdom and richness in our marriage whatever the cost. We're back on the journey.

On July 8, 1994, I wrote out My Pledge, signed and dated it, had it matted and framed, and gave it to Barb for a birthday present. The pledge is this: *"I, Chuck, pledge to love you, Barb, as Christ loved the Church and will lovingly give myself for you should the need ever arise."*

Interestingly enough, that kind of commitment and richness impacts every area of our lives, every relationship we encounter, and the Kingdom of God at large. How? In January of 2002, Barb and I together wrote out, signed, and dated a commitment to God: *"Heavenly Father, we are committed to you in the fulfilling of the Great Commission and offer our lives up to you whatever the cost."* Jesus' grace and richness toward us now results in His grace and richness being expressed through us to others.

Examples: The journey since 2002 has involved two major cancer surgeries for me (I am now cancer free, praise God!) in which Barb was beside me every step of the way. The mission endeavor Christ's Servants to the Nations was founded. We lead a simple church ministry that reaches people of all ages who would never know Jesus if they had to go through the doors of a traditional church to do so—that's part of His grace toward them. The number of such churches is well on the way towards 1,000. We totally trust the Lord for our income, and there is always some to share with others.

In addition to the above, Barb is director of a life-affirming crisis pregnancy center, and I am a hospice chaplain. We both have ample opportunities to share the gospel with people who are open to receiving it. In short, Jesus' ministry of kindness and grace through us has never been more far-reaching, effective, and fulfilling than it is today, and it just keeps growing.

The NIV Compact Dictionary of the Bible describes grace as *"the kindness of God towards men."* There is not a description or category of God's grace that we have not received. We are very much aware that we are recipients of *unmerited favor.* Barb and I are just tremendously blessed.

When we ask, as David did, *"Who are we that you should bless us?"* the only thing we can do is to look back and see that the journey into grace and richness was preceded by another journey—a journey into intimacy.

six

Intimacy and Richness

Sometimes, as Jesus and I journey together, He just starts sharing. Such as…

> Chuck, journeying in richness with Me requires intimacy, and My Word is a record of My yearning for My people to resume intimate relationship with Me.
>
> I create My people for intimacy. I place My whole character and being within them, and I have promised that when their hearts turn cold and stony I will cast out their hearts of sin and put new and loving hearts within them. I will give them hearts of flesh and put My Spirit within them so that intimacy may continue forever.
>
> My desire for intimacy is why I stand at the door of their hearts and knock and if they hear and open I will come in and we will have joyful fellowship together.
>
> My desire for intimacy with you is why I wash not just your feet, but your whole being. I am the vine dresser pruning the branches—I am never nearer than when I am leaning over and pruning in loving, careful, intimate examination making sure that the dead is cut away and that the fruitful is nurtured to even greater richness and abundance.

My desire for rich intimacy with you is why I call you to oneness with Me—I in you and you in Me. The Father calls us both to intimacy—so that He and I together can come in and make ourselves known to you.

My desire to live in intimacy with you is why I went to the cross for you. People do not die for people they are not deeply intimate with or with whom they do not desire a great intimacy. Greater love has no one than that he lay down his life for another. The cross is the only way I could express to you the greatest and most intimate love there is.

Intimacy is the only way that I can live in you and you in Me; therefore, it is the only way that the richness of the kingdom of heaven can become real within you.

Intimacy is why the veil in the temple was rent in half at My crucifixion—so that you could have unhindered access to Me and live in richness with Me.

Marriage between a man and a woman is a visible expression of intimacy with Me. Marriage is why I created man and woman for each other. The way to eternal life is to know the Father in the same way a man and woman *know* each other when they give themselves fully and completely to each other as they are joined together physically, spiritually, and emotionally. *Knowing* requires intimacy.

Only in intimacy with Me...

...do I reveal Myself to you.

...can you bear fruit.

...do you begin to experience a desire to please. The desire to please leads to a desire for obedience, and obedience leads to joy.

...can you adequately discern between darkness and light.

...do you begin to desire to come out of the world.

...can you be made pure and holy and therefore led into all truth.

... will you even begin to know the desire to lay down your life for another.

...can I love you as the Father loves Me, and can you truly love each other. He who does not know the Father does not know love. Again, *knowing* requires intimacy.

...is oneness and completeness possible.

...can we give another our glory.

...can I keep on revealing Myself to you and keep on loving you.

Intimacy is the difference between truly knowing and just being acquainted, between knowing another and using another.

Chuck, only as we are intimate...

...can we rest in each other and experience moments of quiet and peaceful awe with the other.

...can we refresh each other, drink of the overflow of each other's well, or know the pain in each other's heart.

...can we recognize and experience the highest and the holiest in the other.

...does the deep of My heart touch the deep of your heart.

...is there a peace that passes understanding, a knowing that reaches beyond the visible, and a future that stretches from this moment into eternity.

...does the ultimate truly become the ultimate.

Only those who are intimate with Me...

...can enter into the Way, the Truth, the Life

...can see the Father when standing in the presence of the Son.

...will finish well.

...will live in richness with Me.

Intimacy with Me is My gift to you. I bought and paid for this gift on the cross, I testified to the power of this gift at the open tomb. It's a gift. From Me to you. Do you accept or reject? Enter in, or stand apart?

The gift is mine. The choice is yours.

Richness is at stake.

seven

My Response to Jesus' Call to Richness and Intimacy

My responses to Jesus' call to intimacy and richness are,

Worship. Pure and simple worship. No other words or descriptions even come close. The following are some of my personal experiences and expressions of worship:

Awe. Total, complete, unexplainable awe. Overwhelming humility and awe that He considers me worthy of intimacy with Him. I am not worthy, but He is. And that's the difference.

Surrender. Total and complete surrender. Whatever, wherever, however, whenever. I seek to walk in the light as He is in the light. His Word is a lamp unto my feet and a light unto my path.

Worship is now a lifestyle. I worship in spirit and in truth. Worship is no longer a matter of rituals, moments, places, or days. Just a lifestyle.

Life and relationships are *Jesus responses* rather than right or wrong responses. His thoughts are higher than my thoughts and His ways higher than my ways.

Sabbath rest is now a relationship rather than a day. Jesus is my Sabbath, and I rest in Him.

Jesus no longer knocks to come in; He is always in. Sometimes in jubilant celebration, sometimes in peaceful, quiet solitude. Even when tears, trials, and heartaches are present, Jesus always dwells within.

Because I am in Him and He in me fruit is always in process and appropriate to the seasons. Sometimes the seed is being processed and waiting (winter), sometimes being planted (spring), sometimes being cultivated and nurtured (summer), and ultimately being harvested (fall). He, not I, sets the seasons. I simply honor the seasons, and in that I find great richness and peace.

I now live as a person who is completely free. The Son has set me free so I am free indeed. I rest in the knowledge, intimacy, assurance, and freedom of who I am and whose I am.

I totally and completely trust Him for in Him are hidden all the treasures of wisdom and knowledge.

No longer do I ask why. He has assured me that all things work together for good for those who love Him and are called according to His purpose. I surrender to that. His purpose is to mold my character to His character so that through me others see Jesus, know Jesus, become mature and complete in Jesus so that they may be presented to the Father perfect in their relationship to Jesus. And Jesus knows exactly what to allow into my life for all of this to happen.

I am lovingly aware and appreciative of a debt I cannot pay, and I have learned to give up things not worth having in order to gain things I cannot lose.

As the Spirit leads, I frequently pray a prayer of surrender, taught to me by a dear friend who lives every moment in richness with Christ:

> *Lord Jesus, I know that my body is the temple of your Holy Spirit and so I give you permission to move around in me today any way you choose. Work through my mind, see through my eyes, hear through my ears, speak through my lips. Love through my heart, embrace through my arms, serve through my hands. Go with my feet. Supervise and control my thoughts, feelings, actions, and attitudes in ways that give you and the Father the maximum glory. In your name I pray. Amen.*

In summary, living in intimacy with Jesus Christ means that more and more when I think of the wisdom and scope of God's plan, I fall to my knees in awe and surrender and pray to the Father, the Creator of everything in heaven and on earth. I pray that from His glorious, unlimited resources He will give me mighty inner strength through his Holy Spirit. I pray that Christ will be more and more at home in my heart as I trust in Him, and that my roots will go down deep into the soil of God the Father's marvelous love. I pray for the power to understand, as all God's people should, how wide, how long, how high, and how deep His love really is. Intimacy with Jesus results in my longing more and more to experience the unlimited love of Christ, though it is so great I will never fully understand it. And I long to be filled with the fullness of life and power that comes from God, for I know that by his mighty power at work within me, He is able to accomplish infinitely more than I would ever dare to ask or in any way hope on my own. And I pray that God the Father and Jesus the Son be given glory in the church and in Christ Jesus forever and ever through endless ages. Amen.

Intimacy with Christ Jesus begins with an invitation from Christ Jesus, and these are my responses to Him as more and more He molds my character to his character in order that I and others may become mature and complete in Him, and live in richness with Him.

Worship. Everything begins and ends in worship.

eight

Three Essentials to Richness in Christ and Cornerstone Communities

At some point in the Jesus journey you begin to realize that if you are going to live in richness in Christ and be victorious in living a cornerstone life, and establish cornerstone communities, three things are most essential.

Intimacy with Jesus

The first is rich intimacy with Jesus Christ. Jesus says, *"I and the Father are one,"* therefore, you cannot have rich intimacy with God without at the same time having the same intimacy with Jesus.

Intimacy with Others

Secondly, we cannot have pure and complete intimacy with others when we are lacking intimacy with Jesus. The quality and intimacy of our relationship with others, including our husband or wife, is tied directly to the quality and intimacy of our relationship with Jesus. So the second need is rich intimacy with others.

A small band of others who will die for you, if necessary

Thirdly, intimacy with Jesus and others makes way for the third essential—relationship with a small band of other people who would be willing to die for each other if it ever came to that. Why is that needed? Because if you take up the battle of restoring persons, homes, and nations, and if you take up the battle of fighting for other people's hearts, you will at some point be severely attacked. Satan's prime target in attacking you and your work will be your relationships. He will seek to destroy those closest to you first because destroying your close relationships is a great step towards demoralizing, discouraging, and even destroying you. Intimacy with others is a primary defense against attack on the entire cornerstone community.

The price of victory is stated in 1 John 5:4-5: *"...every child of God defeats this evil world by trusting Christ to give the victory. And the ones who win this battle against the world are the ones who believe that Jesus is the Son of God."*

You will not survive the journey without these three things. Walking the Jesus journey, living a cornerstone life, and developing cornerstone communities requires intimacy with Christ, which leads to intimacy with others, which results in that small band of brothers and sisters who would die for each other if the need should ever arise. Without these three things you will not survive the battle. Without rich intimacy with Christ do not even think about joining the battle. To be a leader in this battle for the hearts of others, these things you must do.

Need an example? Try Jesus. He was richly intimate with God the Father. He developed a rich and intimate relationship with a small band of brothers who were willing to die for him if it ever became necessary. And it did. And they did. And it changed the world.

nine

Richness in Christ
and
Finishing Well

It has been said that in the Bible there are over 400 leaders mentioned, but only about eighty of them finished well.

Strong lives, strong homes, and strong nations begin with strong individuals. Everyone who signed the Declaration of Independence, the Constitution, and the Bill of Rights was able to do so because they, as individuals, had their act together. In other words, they knew where they stood with God.

In walking the Jesus journey, living in richness with Christ, and taking cornerstone communities to the homes and the nations of the world, I, Chuck Tooman, need to make sure that God the Father and Jesus the Son are first in my life. I need to be able to say without reservation that Jesus Christ is Lord and Savior of my life. I need to believe, as it says in 1 John 5:4-5:

> For every child of God defeats this evil world by trusting Christ to give the victory. And the ones who win this battle against the world are the ones who believe that Jesus is the Son of God.

And I need to heed the words of the prophet Isaiah that, *"If you do not stand firm for your faith, you will not stand at all"* (7:9).

Some basics. To live that kind of life in whatever role I serve, requires some basics far beyond what the *would-be leader* is willing to adopt. Believe me when I say that there are some basics that, if you make them the center of your being, you can withstand anything the world throws your way on any given day and you will walk in richness with Christ.

Warning! This is not *when I get time* stuff. This is leadership and lifestyle that either you will pay the price or you will simply plop in a puddle. You'll be greatly tempted to compromise at every level. Satan is sly at getting you to think, "Tomorrow is good enough," and that just *thinking* about intimacy in Christ is as acceptable as the reality.

But remember this promise from 1 Corinthians 10:13:

> ... remember that the temptations that come into your life are no different from what others experience. And God is faithful. He will keep the temptation from becoming so strong that you can't stand up against it. When you are tempted, he will show you a way out so that you will not give in to it.

The basics, in addition to seeking a lifestyle of worship, that work for me are as follows:

- Memorize Six Characteristics of God

Omnipotent	Omniscient
Ever Present	Immutable
Immortal	Sinless

- Memorize the Ten Commandments

  1. I am the Lord your God. Do not worship any gods besides me.

2. Do not make idols of any kind.
3. Do not misuse God's name.
4. Remember to honor the Sabbath by keeping it holy.
5. Honor your father and mother.
6. Do not murder.
7. Do not commitment adultery.
8. Do not steal.
9. Do not testify falsely against your neighbor.
10. Do not covet.

- Memorize the Beatitudes (Matthew 5:3-12)

    God blesses those who realize their need for him, for the Kingdom of Heaven is given to them.

    God blesses those who mourn, for they will be comforted.

    God blesses those who are gentle and lowly, for the whole earth will belong to them.

    God blesses those who are hungry and thirsty for justice, for they will receive it in full.

    God blesses those who are merciful, for they will be shown mercy.

    God blesses those whose hearts are pure, for they will see God.

    God blesses those who work for peace, for they will be called the children of God.

    God blesses those who are persecuted because they live for God, for the Kingdom of Heaven is theirs.

    God blesses you when you are mocked and persecuted and lied about because you are my followers.

    Be happy about it! Be very glad! For a great reward awaits you in heaven. And remember, the ancient prophets were persecuted, too.

NOTE: The Beatitudes is the completion side of the Ten Commandments. It is balancing law and love.

- Memorize and wear the armor of spiritual warfare (Ephesians 6:13-18)

  The belt of truth
  The body armor of righteousness
  Shoes of peace, for sharing the Good News
  Shield of faith
  Helmet of salvation
  The Sword of the Spirit, which is the word of God
  Praying in the power of the Holy Spirit

- Live the *Shield of Faith*

  My friend Angela Sedgwick has written,

  > "The shield of faith is an invisible force surrounding Christians from attacks of the devil. The shield of faith is built by believing the truth. When we believe lies instead of truth our shield is weakened and allows evil forces to gain ground in our lives. In order to remain strong in the Lord and protected by His love we must fight the battle of our minds by speaking and claiming what is true. (And always keep in mind that for some reason it is easier to believe lies.) It truly is a war that we're in. We must live by the truth, speak what God says is true, and follow the ways of the Kingdom of God. He is the God of Peace and we can abide in His peace when we are living shielded by faith which is built on truth."

- Memorize Psalm 1

  Focus on at least one scripture verse per week

- Believe that God's Word is totally true and trustworthy.

- Believe that Jesus Christ is God's Son, being totally and completely surrendered to him, and seeking to live every day in intimate communion with him.

- Pray the *Prayer of Divine Surrender*

    Frequently I pray a *Prayer of Divine Surrender*, taught to me by my good friend Bill Bright: Heavenly Father, I know that my body is the temple of your Holy Spirit and so I give you total permission to move around in me any way you choose today. Work through my mind, see through my eyes, hear through my ears, speak through my lips, love through my heart, embrace through my arms, serve with my hands, go with my feet. Take total and complete control, supervise my thoughts, attitudes, action and desires so that you may have the maximum glory. Amen.

- Journal

    Any notebook will do. Simply write down what you have on your heart that you want to tell Jesus. You can also begin by just saying, "Jesus, share with me what's on your heart," and then write down what you feel Him pressing upon your heart.

- Pray the *Prayer of Divine Invitation*

    And then frequently I pray a *Prayer of Divine Invitation* taught to me by another good friend, Robert Fitts: Father, on this day lead me to someone who is hurting or who needs God. Give me the wisdom to know when that happens, and the grace to minister the love of Jesus through the power of the Holy

Spirit. Amen.

- Do them early

    Doing these things at the beginning of my day prepares me with a firm and eternal foundation. Some times I miss a few but essentially these things, plus prayer and scripture, comprise the beginning of my day. Much of it can be done while running, walking, biking, hiking, or whatever else your favorite exercise happens to be.

- Stay in the Word

    First of all, the Word is the Sword of the Spirit. Of all the items of spiritual warfare, the Word is the only offensive weapon. The rest are defensive. Secondly, the Word is sharper than any two-edged sword. If you are not reading the Word then you are fighting with a dull sword! Stay in the Word!

Perfection? Too Holy? Not at all; but neither am I in bondage. What all this does mean is that like King David, when I stumble or fall, I go to my knees in confession and repentance and seek to be restored to the joy of my salvation and the granting of a willing spirit to sustain me. God loved David and David knew it; David also knew that the future of his kingdom depended on a rich relationship with God the Father and His kingdom.

God loves Chuck Tooman, and I know it. I also know that the future of anything He calls me to do depends on a right relationship with him.

ten

Richness and My Core Purpose

One day Jesus asked,

> How well do you understand your purpose?

I was silent. He waited, not needing to fill my silence with words.

> My purpose is to walk with you, to be one with you. Be loyal and faithful to you. Not do things that deny you or undermine you. To live in such a way that others see Christ, know Christ, become mature and complete in Christ so that they may be presented to God the Father perfect in their relationship with Christ.
>
> Chuck, simplify. Just simplify.

"Okay. Like what?"

> First of all, you have it exactly backwards. You have been seeking your purpose and what you can do for me. That's not the way it works. You didn't choose me; I chose you—to go and produce fruit. That's your purpose.

He paused.

"Fruit?"

> *Fruit* is Christ-likeness. Treating people the way I treat them. Remember? "Love the Lord your God with all your heart, soul, mind and strength"? That's Christ-likeness. And when you do for others as you would like them to do for you, that's Christ-likeness. And that's your core-purpose. When you live out your core-purpose, that's bearing fruit. It's fruit that will last. My true followers bear much fruit. That is, they keep growing in their Christ-likeness.

I was silent for awhile. Then, "That's my purpose? Bearing fruit? Growing in treating others the way you treat me? Growing in unconditional love? That's all?!"

> Yes, Chuck. That's all. But be prepared; at some point it may cost you all.

That night I was called to the bedside of a dying man. His only living relative, a niece who lives richness in Christ, and who had come a thousand miles to be with him, sat tearfully and lovingly beside him. I entered into her pain and also shared her joy that her uncle was going to be with Jesus. I held her hand, gave her a hug, tenderly stroked the arms and brow of the dying man. A few minutes later I began reading scripture and praying over the comatose man and his grieving niece who loved him so much. And in the midst of a verse, Jesus laid on my heart, "Chuck, this is fruit-bearing. You entered in and shared me. Your presence is revealing my presence more fully. This is what I mean by fruit-bearing. This is richness in Christ. This is what I called you to do. This is your core purpose."

Later that night the man died, and on my way home, like Jesus' mother I pondered many things in my heart.

eleven

Cornerstone Communities and the Shield of Faith

Let's revisit the shield of faith. The shield of faith is an invisible force surrounding Christians from attacks of the devil. The shield of faith is built by believing the truth. When we believe lies instead of truth our shield is weakened and allows evil forces to gain ground in our lives. In order to remain strong in the Lord and protected by His love we must fight the battle of our minds by speaking and claiming what is true. (And always keep in mind that for some reason it is easier to believe lies.) It truly is a war that we're in. We must live by the truth, speak what God says is true, and follow the ways of the Kingdom of God. He is the God of Peace and we can abide in His peace when we are living shielded by faith which is built on truth. —*God's Message to Angela Sedgwick*

The Jesus Journey Never Ends

Once Jesus has called you to journey with Him, and once you have begun to experience richness in Christ, you will soon discover that the task of fighting for the hearts of others never ends. The shield of faith is built by believing the truth.

There is an enemy who wishes to destroy your heart and does everything he can to destroy the hearts of others. That's why Jesus not only paid the price on the cross at Calvary, but just as importantly arose from the grave to conquer both sin and death and, in essence, to conquer and live victoriously over everything the enemy has to throw at you. The shield of faith is built by believing the truth.

Jesus has called you to journey with Him in restoring hearts, transforming lives, and setting people free. He has called you to richness in Him and with Him. The journey never ends, the enemy never quits, but Jesus is always victorious. The shield of faith is built by believing the truth.

You are Not Alone

You are not on this journey alone. There are others who are leading other Cornerstone Communities, and there are millions who are searching for richness in Christ and a place to belong. There are resources in the persons of prayer who journey with you, worship with you, fellowship and delight in being with you. Your richness in Christ is a constantly renewing and ever-expanding experience in intimacy with Jesus and others. In the good times and the bad, you are never alone. You can do all things through Christ who strengthens you. The shield of faith is built by believing the truth.

twelve

Richness in Christ and Church Pure and Holy

When it comes to experiencing richness in Christ, I don't know that there is anything more beautiful, precious and wonderful than church pure and holy watched over, nurtured, breathed upon and loved upon by God's Holy Spirit, who is also pure and holy. I am talking here about church in all its purity and simplicity.

Ekklesia, translated *church*, was a familiar word in Jesus' day. It was not a religious term. From the Fifth Century BC onwards it referred to the regular assembly of citizens in a city to decide matters affecting their welfare (Acts 19:32,39,41 are excellent examples). *Ekkelsia* (Church) usually meant *gathering*, community or congregation. People of Jesus' day, especially the Greeks, were familiar with the term. It was used to describe people getting together at a multitude of places during their daily lives. Again, it was not a religious term; it was a secular term.

Jesus said, "I will build my church," meaning congregation or community, a gathering of followers. He further stated that wherever two or three were gathered in His name He would be among them. He told the disciples that after He left the earth His Spirit would be with them. His physical presence would be missing but His Spirit would be there in the fullness of His love, power, forgiveness, compassion and all else about Him.

For example, two of Jesus' followers were walking along the road to Emmaus and suddenly Jesus was there with them. As they traveled together, sought truth together, and were in community with one another they experienced *church*—a wonderfully rich and blessed community of spirits together in the presence of Jesus.

The number one place where Barb and I experience church, the beauty and the simplicity of the pure and holy, is right here in our own home. And that is as it should be. Home is the foundation of our daily lives; it is where the Lord nurtures us as He prepares us to go into the world; and it is where His love is first made known more fully and deeply.

God created the first man and woman, Adam and Eve, for each other, gave them to each other, and then provided a most beautiful home setting that they might live together in that setting for eternity. And everyday, in the cool of the day, God came walking by that they might have fellowship with Him and know Him more fully. Church. Pure and holy.

Barb and I experience church pure and holy in our home 24/7 because what goes on here is done in an atmosphere of love and holiness, seeking always to love God with all our heart, soul, mind, and strength. We seek to live a lifestyle of worship.

Sin does not reign in our lives; we are not in bondage to the evil one. Our purity and holiness are a gift from God through the soul-cleansing blood of the *Sacrificial Lamb*, Jesus Christ, who has washed us and made us clean through His everlasting blood covenant. There are days and moments when every bit of the fruit of the Spirit—love , peace, joy, patience, kindness, goodness, and all the rest—is challenged fiercely by the one who seeks always to steal, kill, and destroy. But, the cleansing and the forgiveness are there should we for whatever reason fall into sin.

But even then, even in the midst of the stressful and destructive, Barb and I are still gathered in His name, and it is His Spirit that always prevails. 1 John 5:4-5 tells us that those who win the battle against the world are those who believe that Jesus is the Son of God. All of that, too, is part of church—two or three gathered in Jesus' name regardless of the surroundings.

Things that help church pure and holy to happen here in our home are simple. We have praise and worship music playing in the background almost all our waking hours. Satan finds it difficult to operate in an atmosphere of worship when the worship is not about him. We begin our day with prayer, scripture and devotions, and then pray with each other by phone sometimes during the day. Our offerings go to help support missionaries, feed the hungry, clothe the naked, and help the needy in whatever way the Spirit leads. We also daily share communion.

Sometimes others join us for simple church pure and holy. We laugh, play, cry, work, sing, pray, hike, bike, minister to the dying and the lonely and the desperate, help people move, eat, and more together, with the Spirit pure and holy among us. And that is church.

As I write this I just have received a phone call from the caregiver of a man who is dying. I will go there and we three will be there surrounded by the Holy Spirit and that will be church.

Tonight some of our children and grandchildren will be here for dinner. There will be joy and sharing around the table. There will be thanksgivings shared. That will be church.

Tomorrow morning I will meet with a group of guys at a restaurant for breakfast and we will share what God has done in our lives this past week, including time for accountability. We'll discuss scripture we have read during the week, and pray together. That is church.

Some night next week we will all get together and go Christmas caroling. That will be church pure and holy.

Church pure and holy begins in the home and moves into the world, teaching all nations what Jesus has taught us.

Caution: friends and others will sometimes be very cautious about church pure and holy (or *home churching* as they sometimes call it). Fact: there are millions of people out there who are hungering and thirsting for the things Jesus has to offer but they will never find Jesus if they have to go through the doors of a traditional church to do so.

If your heart is hungry and searching for more, I encourage you to seek and nurture church pure and holy in all its preciousness and simplicity. It is indeed an essential part of your richness in Christ.

thirteen

A Simple Plan for Experiencing Richness in Christ with Others

Another approach to church pure and holy

Jesus said, "Where two or three are gathered in my name, I am there in the midst of them." That's church, gathering. Church is not a place; it is relationship—with Christ and each other.

House2House Magazine (www.house2house.net) offers this short article titled "What Is Simple Church"?

> Simple Church is about a way of life. It is not about a change of location, but about the way we do church. Here are some of the key components to keep in mind:
>
> **FOOD** When you get together, eat! It provides a great atmosphere for people to have open, honest communication with each other.
>
> **OPEN PARTICIPATION** "Well, my brothers and sisters, let's summarize what I am saying. When you meet, one will sing, another will teach, another will tell some special revelation God has given, one will speak in an unknown language, while another will interpret what is said. But everything

that is done must be useful to all and build them up in the Lord" (1 Corinthians 14:26). The key is "everyone has..." Everybody should be able to participate.

BIBLE STUDY Keep it simple and interactive. A great technique is to look over a few verses together and then share what each person has learned.

PRAYER "They joined with the other believers and devoted themselves to the apostles' teaching and fellowship, sharing in the Lord's Supper and in prayer" (Acts 2:42). Find out what is happening in each other's lives and take the time to pray for each other. Expect God to move powerfully and to speak to the group as you pray.

SIMPLICITY Make sure that whatever you do can be duplicated. If the church is going to multiply rapidly, it must be kept simple.

Church is not about the weekly gathering; it is about a different way of life. "And every day, in the Temple and in their homes, they continued to teach and preach this message: 'The Messiah you are looking for is Jesus'" (Acts 5:42).

All of the fore-going have come together today, early in the 21st century, to make the simple church movement the single largest movement in the church worldwide, and millions are experiencing richness in Christ in a way they had never considered possible before.

Want to know more? Somewhere close to you are people who can help you explore simple church in your community. And...there are probably more people around you than you realize who are interested in such an experience and relationship. At the end of this publication is a partial listing of resources for learning more about simple church and issues related thereto.

fourteen

Sustaining Richness in Christ

A canopy of worship over all you do and are

We in America are in very grave danger of losing everything we have. Our cities are subject to terrorist attacks. Traditional values are being scoffed at, disregarded, even trashed under what some consider to be more up-to-date, relevant values and lifestyles. Our Christian faith is increasingly attacked, even silenced in places by those who think they have a better idea.

Traditional family values, including the sanctity of marriage and life, are openly violated and ruled unconstitutional by some courts. Sexual integrity, personal integrity, integrity at any level, is under attack from almost every quarter.

Churches more and more are compromising God's Word, worshiping God, and walking in God's ways in favor of whatever is popular and brings in both people and dollars.

None of this pleases God. It is worshiping gods other than the One True God, building idols, misusing God's name, and giving up the sacred in favor of the profane.

God is not happy, and God will not allow this to continue without a God-response. There is always a price for mocking God and the things God holds dear (Galatians 6:7). It has been true of every generation in the past; God will not make an exception for us.

Only the richness of our intimacy with Christ can change these things.

One goal of Cornerstone Communities is to promote a *canopy of worship* over every home and every community in America. Why? Because evil cannot operate in an atmosphere of worship when that worship is of the Most High God.

Developing a *canopy of worship* over a home and a community will greatly impact a community's culture, values, and lifestyle. It will render us unsusceptible to the enemy's attacks at every level. How do we know that? Because one of God's promises (just one among many promises) is "and he will give you all you need from day to day if you live for him and make the Kingdom of God your primary concern" (Matthew 6:33).

Worship involves exalting God above all else. It involves confessing our failures and selfishness to God and seeking His forgiveness. It involves changing our attitudes and lifestyles and living in ways that truly honor God.

Cornerstone Communities is dedicated to building a canopy of worship over every community in America, and ultimately over America itself that God may protect us from both our enemies and ourselves.

A Plan

1. Pray, asking God's plan for your community.
2. Invite others to pray with you.
3. Establish your home as a home or praise and worship
4. Then, begin developing a home of praise and worship in each block of the community.
5. From there? Wherever God leads.

Visionary? Yes. Will it work? Yes. How do we know? Because God has promised that that which is totally dedicated to Him, honors and glorifies Him, will succeed. Bill Gass, writing in *The Word for You Today* says, "For it is God who works in you to will and to act according to His good purpose (Philippians 2:13 NIV). You may be flawed and limited, but the God who lives and works in you is not! Go ahead, risk, reach, for it is God who works in you."

Henry J. Taylor reminds us that

> Vision lit every lamp, built every church and business, performed every act of kindness, and created more and better things for more people. It's the priceless ingredient of a better day.
>
> Commit to the Lord whatever you do, and your plans will succeed (Proverbs 16:3 NIV).

Many around us are wringing their hands and wondering, "What can I do to help turn this nation around?" Well, here is a most simple plan. It can begin with just you: 24 hours of praise and worship music in your home. Seek first God's face and He will lead you to others who have the same heart and cry for America that you have.

Canopies of praise and worship over communities will eventually result in a *canopy of praise and worship* over our nation. Proverbs 14:34 states, "Godliness exalts a nation, but sin is a disgrace to any people."

Note these words from Psalm 33.

> What joy for the nation whose God is the LORD. . . (vs. 12).
>
> But the LORD watches over those who fear him, those who rely on his unfailing love. He rescues them from death and keeps them alive in times of famine. We depend on the LORD alone to save us. Only he can help us, protecting us like a shield. In him our hearts rejoice, for we are trusting in his holy name. Let your unfailing love surround us, LORD, for our hope is in you alone.(vss. 18-22).

May the Lord's blessings fall gently and joyfully upon your canopy, and may you rejoice without end in your richness in Christ.

fifteen

Richness in Christ and the Power of the Blood of Jesus

In an earlier chapter I said that if you follow the practice of beginning your day grounded in the Word and the Spirit, you will be ready for anything the enemy sends your way during that day.

I turn now to the one thing that is above all else, the pinnacle, the culminating reality and power in our richness in Christ, and that is the power of the blood of Jesus.

Every day Barb and I begin our day with communion. We are both in high profile situations that make us running targets for the enemy. Barb is executive director of a life-affirming pregnancy center located next door to Planned Parenthood. The spiritual warfare against the members of the staff and volunteers and their families and other loved ones is unbelievable.

I serve as a hospice chaplain dedicated to *snatching from the flames* people who have been unbelievers or who have never heard the gospel. On top of that I am a community spokesman for Jesus Christ writing letters to the editor, developing community prayer ministries, leading the development of simple church ministries and healing ministries, and training other leaders to move in the same directions.

We both are dedicated to helping develop mission outreaches both nationally and internationally through Christ's Servants to the Nations, and are the contact persons in Marquette County for Michigan Christian Citizens Alliance. Enough events have happened to both of us that there is no doubt in either of our minds that Satan has an agenda to *take us out* or at least render us ineffective.

In Revelation 12 there is that great battle between Michael and the angels on one hand and the Accuser (Satan) and his angels on the other hand. Verse 12 reads, "And they [the faithful]...defeated him [Satan] by the blood of the lamb and because of their testimony."

Derek Prince, in *Spiritual Warfare*, suggests that our testimony centers in two things: "The Word of God and the blood of Jesus. [Our] testimony releases the power that is in the Word and the blood."

1 Corinthians 11: 26 says, "For every time you eat this bread and drink this cup, you are announcing the Lord's death until he comes again."

Each morning when Barb and I share Holy Communion we are proclaiming not only our Lord's death but also the power of His resurrection. Therefore, the blood becomes not only a hedge of protection but also an offensive weapon whereby we go into the day knowing that everything that comes our way during the day is subject to the power of the cross and the promise of the resurrection.

> No, despite all these things, overwhelming victory is ours through Christ, who loved us. And I am convinced that nothing can ever separate us from his love. Death can't, and life can't. The angels can't, and the demons can't. Our fears for today, our worries

about tomorrow, and even the powers of hell can't keep God's love away. Whether we are high above the sky or in the deepest ocean, nothing in all creation will ever be able to separate us from the love of God that is revealed in Christ Jesus our Lord (Romans 8:38-39).

Such is the power of the blood of Jesus, and our richness in Christ, at the beginning of our day as well as through out our day.

A Terrible Urgency

I urge you to begin now to seek intimacy with Jesus and live a Cornerstone Life centered on Jesus Christ as the cornerstone. Also begin to develop your home into a Cornerstone Home. In Cornerstone homes ...

- People feel warmly loved, highly valued, deeply respected, greatly encouraged and genuinely supported--even in tough times
- Relationships make a difference and set an example
- People and relationships withstand life's storms
- Dreams, visions and goals are allowed and encouraged
- People bring out the best in each other
- Joy is present, even in the midst of heartaches
- People and relationships are forgiven and restored
- People think and value in terms of eternity, not just the present
- Life is not perfect, but it is very good
- Jesus Christ is the center

Cornerstone Homes are the safest places on earth.

Again, begin now to: (1) seek intimacy with Jesus, (2) live a Cornerstone Life, (3) make your home a Cornerstone Home, (4) invite others to join you in a Cornerstone Community—a small group of people who gather frequently to worship God the Father and Jesus the Son.

Prayer, the Bible, and a willing spirit are all you need to get started. Let the Holy Spirit lead you from here. Begin now. The time is urgent.

Chuck Tooman
Christ's Servant to the Nations
1402 West Avenue
Marquette, MI 49855
USA

Please share this with everyone you know.

Bibliography and other Resources

Books

Dale, Tony and Felicity. *Simple Church.* Karis Publishers, Austin, TX, 2002.

Eldridge, John. *Waking the Dead — the Glory of a Heart Fully Alive.* Thomas Nelson Publishers: Nashville, 2003.

Fitts, Robert. *The Church in the House — A Return to Simplicity.* Preparing the Way Publishers, Salem, OR, 2001.

Fitts, Robert. *Forty Trends Back to Simplicity.* Kona, HI, 2005.

Krupp. Nate. *God's Simple Plan for His Church.* Preparing the Way Publishers, 2003.

Rutz, Jim. *Mega Shift — the Best News Since Year One.* Empowerment Press, Colorado Springs, CO, 2005.

Rutz, Jim. *Open Church.* Seed Sowers Publishers, Beaumont, TX, 1992.

Rutz, Jim. *The Rebirth of the Church.* Seed Sowers Publishers, Beaumont, TX, Second Edition, 1994.

Stedman, Ray. *Body Life.* Discovery House Publishers, Grand Rapids, MI, Revised Edition, 1995.

Viola, Frank. *Pagan Christianity.* Present Testimony Ministries, Gainesville, FL, 2002.
Viola, Frank. *Rethinking the Wineskin.* Present Testimony Ministries, Gainesville, FL, 2001.
Viola, Frank. *The Untold Story of the New Testament Church.* Present Testimony Ministries, Gainesville, FL, 2003.
Zdero, Rod. *The Global House Church Movement.* William Carey Library, Pasadena, CA, 2004.

Websites

www.house2house.net
www.robertfitts.com
www.chucktooman.com
www.allaboutgod.com
www.cofcare.org
www.dawnministries.org

Workshop, Training and Conference Resources

Robert Fitts
Outreach Fellowship International
76-6309 Haku Place
Kailua-Kona, HI 96740
Website: www.robertfitts.com
Phone: 808-334-9682/808-371-6338

Chuck Tooman
Christ's Servants to the Nations
1402 West Avenue
Marquette, MI 49855
email: cbtooman@yahoo.com
Website: www.chucktooman.com
Phone: 906-228-3788

Other PTWP Books that will help you experience Richness in Christ

Foundations for the Christian Life
by John G. Gill

Written to give the foundation stones for the Christian life, as listed in Hebrews 6:1-3. Many Christians struggle in their Christian life because the proper foundation was not laid in the beginning. This book biblically gives this proper foundation. Questions at the end of each chapter make it even more practical.

ISBN 1-929451-11-3 • 124 pages $11.95

God's Word Puts the Wind in My Sails
by Joanne Bachran

A guide to knowing GOD and His Word. It is full of helpful, basic material for all believers, especially new Christians. A reference guide, Bible study, personal devotional, and journal—all rolled into one. A personal compass for a more intimate relationship with God. Very useful!

ISBN 1-929451-08-3 • 216 pages $13.95

Woman—God's Plan not Man's Tradition
by Joanne Krupp

Examines every major passage in the Bible on the subject of God's plan for women. It refutes the traditional teaching of husbands having authority over their wives and of a limited role for women in the Church. It biblically releases women to become all that God intends them to be as equal partners in the home and the Church. The conclusions of this book need to be prayerfully considered by all—men and women!

ISBN 1-929451-00-8 • 156 pages $11.95

God's Simple Plan for His Church— and Your Place in It
by Nate Krupp

A radical look at God's biblical plan for His Church—what the New Testament really teaches about the Church! A manual for house churches that is being used on every continent. The text remains the same in this 2nd edition—helpful information in the appendices has been updated.

ISBN 1-929451-12-1 • 184 pages $11.95

The Church in the House—a Return to Simplicity
by Robert Fitts

This is another classic on the subject of home church. Evangelize the world quickly by planting millions of house churches everywhere. This book tells you how. Earlier editions of this book have already gone around the world. We are thrilled to be able to publish this new, revised edition.

ISBN 1-929451-07-5 • 120 pages $9.95

Knowing GOD Series *from Preparing the Way Publishers*

The Knowing GOD Series consists of five study books. Each one takes you deeper in your knowledge of God's Word and in your relationship with Him. You do not need to do the series in the given order (1-5), but you may find that helpful.

#1 Basic Bible Studies
   ISBN 1-929451-02-4 • 80 pages $11.95

A question-and-answer type, foundational Bible study book about the Christian faith. Chapters include:

1. Is There a God?
2. The Issue of Sin
3. What Provision Did God Make For Man's Sin?
4. How Should Man Respond to God's Provision?
5. Abiding in Christ
6. The Christian and God's Word
7. The Christian and Prayer
8. The Christian and the Holy Spirit
9. The Christian and Warfare
10. The Christian and Witnessing
11. The Christian and the Home
12. The Christian and the Church
13. The Christian and Business Affairs
14. The Christian and Discipleship
15. The Christian and Service
16. The Christian and the Return of Christ

#2 New Testament Survey Course
   ISBN 1-929451-03-2 • 234 pages $19.95

This is a very unique 47-lesson Bible study survey of the New Testament.

- It covers every verse of the New Testament
- It leads you in an in-depth study of each book. You will read the entire New Testament and either answer summarizing questions or summarize the book, a paragraph at a time.
- It harmonizes the Gospels so that you study Jesus' life in a single, chronological narrative.
- It places the letters in the order in which they were actually written.
- This study gives you background information on each book of the New Testament.
- You will apply each book to your own life situation.
- You will decide on verses to memorize from each book.
- You will know the New Testament when you have finished this study!

#3 Mastering the Word of God - and Letting It Master You!
   ISBN 1-929451-04-0 • 46 pages $6.95
   Workbook • ISBN 1-929451-09-1 • 34 pages $5.95
This book is about various methods of in-depth Bible intake: how to hear, read, study, memorize, and meditate on the Word of God. With this book you will learn how to study the Bible. You will be able to develop a life-long plan of in-depth Bible study - mastering God's Word, and letting It master you.
   Bible Outlines • ISBN 1-929451-10-5 • 62 pages... $9.95

#4 Getting to Know GOD
   ISBN 1-929451-05-9 • 288 pages $23.95
A devotional Bible study book on 57 aspects of GOD's Person, Character, and Attributes: His love, His mercy, His faithfulness, His goodness, His glory and majesty, etc. For each attribute, you will read an introduction, prayerfully read three or four pages of appropriate Scripture verses, answer study questions, do research, meditate on and apply the lesson to your life, memorize verses of your choice, and pray a closing prayer. This book was written by an actual Bible study group. This study will change your life!

#5 Qualities God is Looking for in Us
   ISBN 1-929451-06-7 • 384 pages $29.95
A 53-week Bible study, devotional book on the qualities God is looking for in us: abiding in Christ, boldness, contentment, diligence, discipline, early riser, forgiving, generous, holy, honest, humble, obedient, praiser, prayer, servant, wise, zealous, etc. For each quality, you will read an introduction, prayerfully read three or four pages of appropriate Scripture verses, answer study questions, do research, meditate on and apply the lesson to your life, memorize verses of your choice, and pray a closing prayer. This book was written by an actual Bible Study group. This study will greatly challenge you!

Order Form Next Page

ORDER FORM
Preparing the Way Publishers
2121 Barnes Avenue SE, Salem, OR 97306, USA
Voice 503-585-4054 • Fax 503-375-8401
E-mail: kruppnj@open.org • Website: www.PTWpublish.com

QTY	TITLE	PRICE	TOTAL
_____	Foundations for the Christian Life	$11.95	_____
_____	God's Word Puts the Wind in My Sail	$13.95	_____
_____	Woman—God's Plan Not Man's Tradition	$11.95	_____
_____	God's Simple Plan for His Church	$11.95	_____
_____	The Church in the House	$9.95	_____

KNOWING GOD SERIES

QTY	TITLE	PRICE	TOTAL
_____	#1 Basic Bible Studies	$11.95	_____
_____	#2 New Testament Survey Course	$19.95	_____
_____	#3 Mastering the Word of God	$6.95	_____
_____	Workbook	$5.95	_____
_____	Bible Outlines	$9.95	_____
_____	#4 Getting to Know GOD	$23.95	_____
_____	#5 Qualities GOD is Looking for in Us	$29.95	_____

Ordering Information: Fill in your order and send it **with payment** to Preparing the Way Publishers for processing. A new copy of this Order Form will be included with your order for your future ordering use.

Payments: To avoid extra bookkeeping and handling expenses, credits for less than $1.00 will not be sent. Prices are subject to change without notice. **Full payment is expected with order.**

Postage and Handling for mainland United States orders:

Amount of Order	P & H	Postage and Handling for Alaska, Hawaii,
Under $20.00	$4.00	U.S. possessions, and all other nations:
$20.00 - $39.99	15%	Actual postage charge plus 10% handling
$40.00 and above	10%	

            TOTAL Book Order $ _____

            Plus Postage & Handling $ _____

            GRAND TOTAL $ _____

Ship To:

Name: _____ Date of Order: _____

Address: _____ Telephone: _____

City _____ State _____ Zip _____ Nation _____

✂ Clip and mail

Preparing the Way Publishers

makes available practical materials
(books, booklets, and audio tapes)
that call the Church to the radical Christianity
described in the Bible.

Some titles include —
The Way to God
Basic Bible Studies
New Testament Survey Course
Mastering the Word of God — and Letting It Master You
Bible Outlines
Getting to Know GOD
Qualities God is Looking for in Us
Bible Studies for Soul Winners
You can be a Soul Winner — Here's How!
The Church Triumphant at the End of the Age
New Wine Skins — the Church in Transition
God's Simple Plan for His Church — a Manual for House Churches
Leadership–Servanthood in the Church as found in the New Testament
Woman — God's Plan not Man's Tradition
Restoring the Vision of the End-times Church
God's Word Puts the Wind in My Sail
Foundations for the Christian Life

For further information, see the PTW web page
at www.PTWPublish.com

Or contact —

Preparing the Way Publishers
2121 Barnes Avenue SE
Salem, OR 97306-1096, USA

phone 503/585-4054
fax 503/375-8401
e-mail <kruppnj@open.org>

MANCHESTER COLLEGE LIBRARY

3 9315 01043719 9

248.4 T618r
Tooman, Chuck.
Richness in Christ

DATE DUE

WITHDRAWN
from
Funderburg Library

Printed in the United States
49314LVS00002B/4-54

9 781929 451203